LOVE EVERY THING

POEMS FOR SUBMERGING IN THE INFINITE OCEAN OF LOVE

akasha

Art & Cover design by David Provolo Copyright © 2025
Editing by Sage Taylor Kingsley www.SageforYourPage.com

Paperback ISBN: 979-8-9996236-0-7
Ebook ISBN: 979-8-9996236-1-4

First Edition

Published by Blue Heron Creations, LLC
7990 SW Boeckman Rd,
Wilsonville, OR 97070,
USA

Contact
https://linktr.ee/drakasha

for dakari,
it's okay to love as deeply as you do.
and for you, who feel called to experience
a soak in something vaster and deeper.

contents

preface

this book of poems is an accident that was meant to happen. you know, like people you know who have children late (or very early) in life. my amazing son was not planned. i am so happy he was born. like that. i did not set out to write poems. i am more of an accidental poet. and this book is like the site of 144 of those accidents.

in 2016, three questions arrested my attention and my energy:
- who am i, really?
- why am i here?
- who is god, for me? (not based on any sacred book or guru's words)

i bumped into the answers to those three questions while walking the camino de santiago pilgrimage later that year. and following that, my meditation practice delivered me, metaphorically, literally, and metaphysically, into the infinite ocean of love, and i've not ventured out since. it's a cool place.

so, i packed up all my *nothings* from the world and moved in. since then, i have been diving deeper into my experience of the divine, surrender, and—you guessed it—love.

i have a perspective that poets have given themselves over to love: love of life, love of truth, love of the divine, love of justice, love of humanity, love of nature, love of love. and not just poets. all of us are such lovers. you are such a lover. why else would you pick up this book?

i wonder, though, if you have your lover hiding in the closet of past hurts, or future expectations? perhaps you are reading these very words because it is now time for you to open that door, to open your heart even more than you imagined possible. what if words can be more than words?

words can harm or help, can heal and harmonize.

words are also containers for energy, for love.

may you experience these words as a gentle pool of love.

come.

have your own accident with love.

dive in.

love everything,

akasha

flirting

in the beginning,
and now,
we are
the idea
the universe
is thinking,
the word
the holy one
is speaking.
we are a
divine poem,
sweet words
spoken from
the mouth
of god.

go look.
yes.
and find yourself
resting inside
your own heart.

wherever you are going in life,
the best way to get there
is to fly first class on divine air.
it's immediate. reliable. definite.
every flight is
light on time.
plus, there's no baggage to claim.
now, *that's* traveling in style.

everywhere,
mind mucks busily,
exposing its purpose.
just now,
it stumbled into me.
it was love at first bump
there is no doubt:
we were made for each other.
now, my existence is married
to life's cause.

grounded,
you make
all things
perfect, oh,
divine one.

root me
deep in
the perfection
of your
creation.
plant me,
immovable, in
your garden
of eden.

this game that the
divine plays with us
is a most loving
and rewarding game:
no one loses.
if it feels like
you're losing,
you're likely
just at
half time.
rest and
get back
in the game.
keep playing.

your presence
merges with
the truth of
my being
and reveals
the path
to divine love.

i am learning to maintain
my empty position of self as itself.
so, i sit while sitting
and sit while not sitting.
i refuse to get up
from the posture of
the unfolding reality of life.

walking through
this vast world,
i found
my self sitting.
who is this
fellow walking, then?

do not take a regular path.
do not look for an irregular path.
make your path by choosing
a non-path.
follow the natural
pull of being.

old man sitting in my house,
consciousness.
guiding me to god,
emptiness.
"let go. let go," he said.
holding on to just being,
nothingness.
and now we share the same home,
oneness.

to change
your psychic
address and
move to heaven
on earth,
pave the
road you
walk with
love, and
then dedicate
the road
to the divine.
and after
you've done
all that,
ask her
to be
the only
traveler.

yes, god does have a sense of humor.
and one way to experience it
is to think,
"that's impossible"
 or "no one loves me."

yes. that will surely
make god laugh so hard,
that water will pour from the skies

drenching you
in an outpouring
of love drops.

now that
you have
said yes
to something new,
something beyond
the realm
of your
just-now
reality,

you have
become a stranger
to yourself,
a stranger
to your
once-familiar world.

now that
you have
said yes,
welcome this
secret resident
of your self
who has
been knocking,
for eons,
from the inside,
of the door
of your awareness,

whispering: *let*
me out,
god damn it!
let me
be free.
let me
be you,
for buddha's sake.

and finally,
suddenly, and
without warning—
you comply.

welcome this stranger,
to yourself.
welcome, oh,
self of
the divine one.
welcome om.

this whole
existence is
like a mega
concert that
the divine
puts on
just for us.

and we're
like: *where
is the venue?
where do
i get tickets?
what shoes
should i wear?*

just stop!

stop!

the concert
is already
happening
right now,
right where you are,
just for you.

so, tune in.

listen.
dance.
sing along.

and then
go home
with the
main attraction.

it will
be the
best love
you've ever had.

back,
back,
within myself.
like entering the vast depths
of a tunnel
while facing the one light of many
worlds.
coming to rest,
yes,
in a new home that has claimed me
as its own.
somewhere between
seeing the light
and being embraced by the dark.
at home now,
in the glimmering
shadowy depths of the self.

can i manage
to be empty long enough
to discover life's expressions
and then reflect its revelations?
no.
not until all my efforts are
given back to life itself.

i am suspended
over an abyss
of the great unknown,
hanging on
to a string of thought
made up of familiarities.
my arms grow weary.
letting go seems risky,
but holding on is so painf—
—wait!
where am i?

introduce your mind
to the present moment.
i can't say that
they'll be friends,
but you'll be free
to experience life eternal.

who knows what tomorrow will bring?
well, tomorrow does,
but it will not tell anyone.
not until you give birth to it
as an act of love.

love,
ever so gently,
smashes me
into 10 billion pieces
to show me
its universal oneness.

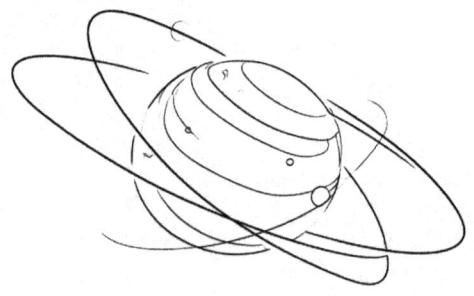

she ordered acceptance
and as the waiter
walked past me
with it
covered up
on a tray,
i could smell it.
i. could. smell. acceptance.

it smelt like …
sniff …
sigh …
like love.

acceptance smells
like love.
and what does
love smell like?

well …
love smells like
a journey down
loss, pain, and suffering.
also, joy. yes, joy, too.
and delight. and wonder.
and surprise.
and the most
intimate mixture of
being seen and being met
that you could ever imagine.

and now.
right now.
this moment.
can you smell that?
that's what love smells like.

as the waiter returned,
empty-handed,
i grabbed his attention,
and demanded,
"i want what
she's having.
double portion."

every soul
you meet—woman, boy
ant, tree, soil—
is a
divine sign
that reads:
this way
to god.
pay attention.
follow the signs.
do not
miss a turn.
else, you get
lost and
have to
start all
over again.

i sit naked before you,
empty.
all i have to offer is
infinite nothingness.

the wisdom
of infinite love
is found
in being
a fool for you,
oh, wise one.

when i kissed
your feet
this morning,
all the heavens
kissed me back.
funny.
i never thought
that i would find
god so low.

rushing ahead
of love,
i missed the
taste of
the most
delicious connection.
now, i'm
learning to savor
the feast
of each moment.
mmmm.
yummy.

did you hear that sound?
the divine is
standing at
your heart
with a
holy hammer,
ready.
ready to
strike your
one heart
wide open.
best you
get out
of the
way.
because she
will smash
your entire
being to
everythingness.

the universe
stands before you,
everywhere,
naked,
baring itself
freely before
your eyes.

i mean ...

look at
the ocean.
look at
the fire.
look at
the earth.
look at
the sky.
look at
the air.

all naked.

do not
avert your gaze.
there is
no shame
in this.

now,
all that's
left to
do is
to fall
into the universe's
naked embrace.

and feel free
to make love.

p.s. don't tell
anyone that
i suggested this.
or they'll tell us to get a room,
and a love like ours can't fit in there.

courting

every now and zen,
i take my mind out
and put it in my pocket.
finally!
i can walk around more mindfully.

seeing you last night,
dear cosmic dancer,
released me from
1,000 ways
of hiding from your love.
no more hiding.
as rhythmless as i am,
accept me as your student.

the joy of my existence
is surrendering "my"
and being swallowed up by love.
day after day.
and it's not only me.
love swallows up all people and all things.
she has an insatiable appetite.

looking beyond the
sun's light,
i see his
warm face,

beyond the
river's flow,
her embracing
arms,

beyond my
beating heart,
the all-loving
divine.

the path to being
passes egoism
intersects with awakening
flows into emptying
and continues along, serving.

when i
dance to
sacred chants,
it's like
the divine
has made
me his
dance floor,
then his
dance partner,
then his
dancing body,
as he
moves inside,
from ground
to heart.

and yet,
i desire
him to
move in
even closer.
yes, closer.
closer than
inside.

in solitude,
the past and future
would deafen my peace,
if not for the mute button
activated by timeless presence.

life is
like a playlist.
start the music
and then
step back,
allow the
universe to
be the dj.
then simply
dance when
life plays.

if your
current dwelling
place is
not ideal,
move into
love.
love is
the best
place to
live. and
love makes
the uncomfortable
tolerable
and the
tolerable, divine.

sitting at
spirit's bar,
i ordered
a shot
of presence.

that's the
last thing
i remembered.

just a glass,
and i'm forever
intoxicated with
divine love.

now, i
must prepare
myself for
an endless hangover.

last night i consumed
too much of the
divine's love.
now, i can hardly
think hate,
care less,
or avoid
clearing a dam
to the
divine's love.
and that
was after only
10 minutes
with her.

i have wondered:
what do
the sun, clouds,
and air
say to each other
to produce such
spectacular art
on the sky's canvas?
and what does
the shore
say to
the ocean
to keep
her coming back
to smooth
his rough edges?
and what do
the bones and cells
say to my body
to hear your whispers
from a thousand thousand
lifetimes away
to make space to welcome
the universe itself?
who knows?
and what do i
need to say to you

that you always knew
but need to remember?
last night
i was minding
my own business
when love
snuck up
on me,
pulled me
into itself.
it was
a full
merger and acquisition.
now,
i have
no business
to mind.
love has
it all.

when you
see me
ranting and raving,
dancing with myself,
up all night
writing love letters
to god,

yes, i've
gone crazy,
no doubt.

and you
have permission
to institutionalize me.

yes, i'm serious.
lock me up.

lock me up
in love.
and no visitation rights please.

leave me
and love alone.
unless, of course, you
want to dance with us.

i'm like
the bed
of a river
being filled
up with the
presence of
your energy.

flow in me,
liquid spirit.
drown me
in the depths
of your love.

there is a
shortcut
to the divine:
stop thinking
stop talking
start dancing

and you're there.

oh, divine
one, i'll
forever be
your mouth
piece, your body
part, and your
piece of
mind.

(no need
for a
backup plan).

when life's music plays,
the divine thrums my
heart like a guitar,
shakes my body like maracas,
beats my mind
like a drum,
and blows my
breath like a flute.
it feels so good
to be played
and a player
in the divine's
orchestra.

at sunrise,
i am baptized in
the infinite ocean of love.

at midday,
i sit on my cushion and
disappear into emptiness.
by nightfall,
i have climbed the eight limbs
to rest in shiva's bosom.
and that's not
the end of it.
no, beloved,
no, no.
sometimes i am up
at midnight.
and if you peek inside
the window of my soul,
you will likely see me
whirling nonstop to the
rhythms of love.

everywhere i turn,
you are there.
i am not complaining,
but i do wonder if you
ever get bored
of following
yourself around.

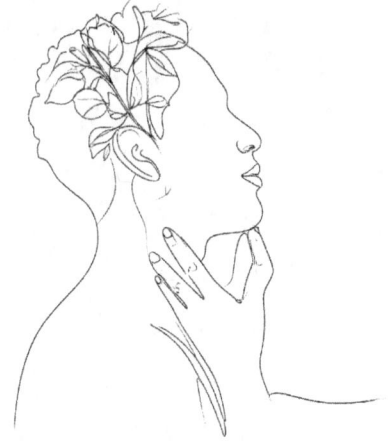

i saw who's been
staying over at
your place a lot lately.

how blessed you are
to wake up to
that glorious
presence every day!

i should warn you though:
he sleeps around.
a lot.
8 billion and counting.

everything inside
this estate—
the life,
the thoughts,
the emotions,
the love,
the power,
the purpose,
the motivations—
are all yours.

you are
the sole
estate owner,
oh, divine
one.

mark your
boundary around
me so
that
all others
may know:

"no funny business allowed."

what lies active and true,
but suppressed,
in the bosom of the soul,
will one day
burn down the
walls in the mind
to find expression.
wait on that day.
or choose now
to set the contents of
your soul free.

i relax the muscles
of the mind
rest the desires
of the heart
and stretch the limbs
of infinite love
to wake up
in the company
of your divinity.

this morning,
i move through the world
in a lotus position,
seeking after life
with all my senses.
i'm like a dog
sniffing every scent
in search of its master.

today,
i left my house
intent on becoming somebody,
on showing the world
just how important i am.
and you wouldn't believe
who i met along the way.

Yes.

the world!
looking lost,
searching for its own importance.
now, i'm on my way back home,
a nobody, with a worldly friend.

when she went away,
she left me with one thing:
she said,
"love is unbound and abundant.
it is your only inheritance."

since then,
i have been burning through it
like there is no tomorrow.

when i empty
and let go,
love fills me up
and liberation
holds my hand.
i see.
all this sitting
and doing nothing
is to make room
for god.

there is
an obvious
symptom whenever
the divine
touches me.
i am
no doctor,
but i
swear the
spot where
she loves
me becomes so
tender and fiery
it's like
ice on fire.

embrace whatever
you reject
about yourself
and you help build
a love storm
that dries every desert
quenches every thirst
and refreshes every heart.

extend your
shackled mind
to the boundless
hand of love.
it holds the solution
to your sure
and final liberation.
so have no doubt.
you cannot
remain locked in thoughts.
not even from
a half-turn
of love's master key
when the turning
creates so much
love vibe ration.

from the space
of seeing choices,
empty.
from the place
of being empty,
love!

take me,
o divine one,
beyond the
gate of surrender.
and leave
the me
right there.
so only
one remains.

he wanted to hold
onto love
but it is like
a wave of cosmic wind
that washes over all.
so he gave up holding
and embraced
being cosmically
loved instead.

you cracked me open
with the hammer of your love,
and swept up my fears
with your all-embracing hands.
now, broken whole and fearless,
i couldn't be any closer to you.

point me
the way
to surrender,
dear divine one.

and when
i arrive
please hold
me and
do not
let me go!

when you
have surrendered
completely to love,
keep surrendering
your surrender.

otherwise you
may forget
just how
loved and
loving you are.

now, surrender
to that.
and surrender
again.

that's it.
that's it ...

four words
hold the
key to
our freedom:

i accept.
thank you.

that's it.
it's that simple.

now, repeat
after me:

i accept.
thank you.

only 107
more times
to go
for today.

i accept.
thank you.

now, we're
down to 106.

you're welcome.

maturing
love

on the road to
discover what you are,
walk out on
who you were.
if you can
perceive the difference,
you are well
on your way.

i looked for me
in the things i do
and found only ideas,
expectations,
and fears.
then i looked
for me beyond me
and found only light
at the bottom
of an all-encompassing
cosmic wave of love.
for a while, i stopped looking.
i lost the sense of me.
it was
ever-evolving,
ever-unfolding.
now, i hear a hint
of a reality
beneath the unfolding,
whispering, "i believe what i am not.
and what i am
is what i have always been."

the divine
has dismembered
the arms
of my
mind, and
now i
have nothing
to grasp
things with,
nothing to
let go of.

for the
first time,
i drank
a cup
of love
from the
divine's hand
and gulped
it down
like a
cold drink
on the
hottest of
summer days.
the thing
that surprised
me is
that even
after my
thirst disappeared,
the cup
remained full.
it was
like love
on tap.

now tell me.
what kind of holy
magic is this?

go ahead,
remove the salt
from the ocean,
the air
from the wind,
and life
from the universe.
only then will you
have discovered
how separate
and alone
we are.
now try to
remove the divine
from your body,
the magic from your breath,
the moonlight from your heart,
the mystery from your essence.

now, do you see?
how separate and
alone we truly are?

the stream of life
flows,
engulfing the material,
overflowing the spiritual,
leaving only the original:
you.

what can resist
the path of
life's singular
purpose of oneness?

dam, mind.

to truly
accept others
is a
result of
loving the
life you
live.
and living the
life you love.

what do you do
when all
you see
is what cannot
be seen?
when what
you can touch
is untouchable?
when you
walk from
soul to soul,
universe to universe
and then see god herself ...
what do you do, huh?
when you
realize that
the stuff
you are
made of
is stardust?
and you
can make
new worlds
with a
single
thought?

do not
run away.
do not hide.
do not
make a fuss
about it either.

just keep
on being cosmic dust.
for someday
that dust
inside you
will re-form into
a most glorious light.
ah. i see it
already has.

they asked me
how and
where and
when i
met the divine.

and all
i could
reply with
was: "now."

so i told them
we met in the now.
being present
to the
misty horizon
of a space beyond time,
beyond intimacy,
and dancing in poetry.

i told them of
how we met inside
the being of our
naked relating.

of how we met
in emptiness,
using silent words that
unlocked the chains that
held our
deepest longing.

in talks of place,
of presence,
of vocation and the
things that matter most.

we met in the
undeniable recognition
that this here is
the awakening
of mutual love.

that is how we met,
i told them.
we met in the
truth of now.
we met in love.

the question isn't
do we have
what we need?
it's:
do we need
what we already have?

and what we have
is a whole universe
inside of us.

god.

life.

abundance.

our life
is one
of subtraction.

we don't
need to
add anything.

everything is
already here
for us.

we remove
ideas of
being unlovable.
we remove
old stories.

we remove
bad beliefs.

we remove
all that
limits us.

and what
remains is
what has
always been here:
life divine.

entering farther
into the dark realm
of the self,
all around
i ses
the jagged edges,
the murky ground,
and the broken might
of my inner world.
now, bruised, dirty, and limping,
i embrace the light
this darkness brings.

excuse my silence,
and my slow
unfolding movement.

i am like
an unborn baby
resting in
the infinite ocean
of love's womb.

when i want to go places,
i grab a cushion,
sit inside my breath,
and move from my head
to my heart
to arrive home
in my self.
best welcome committee ever!

faster than the speed
of my thoughts and actions,
is life's unmoving gift
of freedom.
so, do not go anywhere.

sit here
and be free.

sitting in presence,
i fly through the heavens
like a bird.
i run through the woods
like a wolf.
all this movement and travel,
and going nowhere.

till the ground of the mind.
examine the seeds of all thoughts.

nourish their growth.

uproot them.

cut them down.

ignore them.

all these choices are
in the hands of love,
the master gardener.

in my being,
i learn to touch heaven
and earth,
with the same finger of awareness.

we are:
thought inside
the divine's mind.
love inside
the divine's heart.
and a dream
inside the
divine's soul.
there is no question,
then, about
who belongs
to whom.

now that i am
full of you,
who is also
me, does that
mean i
am a
divine narcissist?
oh, lord!

package received.
stop.
it's perfect.
stop.
thank you.
stop.
i accept.
stop.

nothing in this whole universe
moves faster than
the speed of love.

so, slow down.
breathe.
rest.
love already has won.

do not stand
in the way
of love.
relax your body,
soften your heart,
let go of your thoughts.
be absorbed in
love's ever-present embrace.
be free.
be loverated.

when love calls out,
"who is my favorite one?"
infinite beings form a line
that stretches beyond
even the bounds of time.

i closed my eyes
and in my
naked surrender
emptiness embraced me
and made me love.

i crawl to the edge
of our oneness
and attempt to jump over
into the stream of me-ness,
to live my own life.
i am not alone.

all around me,
billions move as one,
unaware of the edgeless edge ahead
that drops into "my own life."
i surrender.
for us,
there is no
escaping our unity.

with eyes contracted
and thoughts muted,
follow the
gaze of consciousness
as ego is liberated
and the soul elevated.

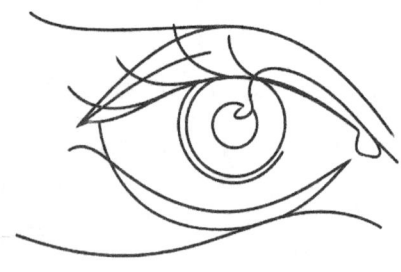

only the heart of
the seen can truly
love another.
for love is made
visible only
when souls
settle themselves
long enough
to be seen and
to see the luminous
presence of the divine
shining through the transparent
eyes of those who see.

you smashed
down the
door of
my heart
with your
quiet entrance and
demanded:
we need
to be lovers.
and now
and then
you refused
to leave.
i think
we need
a bigger place,
oh, divine lover.

it's not standing on
our heads,
walking on hot coals,
or levitating.
no.
it's not sitting
in meditation,
hugging countless trees,
or chanting the million
and one names for god.
no.
these things do
not make us free
or evolved.
they are simply
the feet we
use to
walk upon
the ground
that is
the mind
of the
divine one.
surrender all our efforts
at holiness,
trade in all our desires
for emptiness,
and embrace
the reality of our everything.

performing one
genuine act
of love
for another
human being
subtracts the lies
that lead
to their
root suffering.
understand this
cosmic math
and you
will graduate
human school.
live it daily
and make
the divine's honor roll.

what mistakes?
love is
like a
giant eraser
clearing away
all errors
and any belief
in them.

i saw two rocks
kissing each other
this morning.
i don't know
how they do it
but they just sat there,
frozen.
lips on cheeks,
nowhere to go,
nothing to do.
madame time,
may you also
freeze the expression
of my love
for the divine?
a love frozen in time.

like the mist
from the ocean's
splashing waves reveals
the rainbow's presence,
so the coming
and going of my life
illuminates your light.

devotion is the most
delicate thing.

there is no rush
to anywhere.

groove into it,
allow your
movement to
settle.
and your
spirit to
dance

in the fire
of timelessness.

devotion is
delicate like
a lotus flower.

open your
senses in
slow motion,
take it all in.

then empty yourself
out on
the floor
of the
divine's heart.

be soft
be subtle
be empty
be the space
that holds
your devotion.

devotion is delicate.
devotion is your
engraved invitation
to dance with the divine.

if you love deeply,
your heart
has already
been shattered
into a thousand pieces.
pick up the pieces.
place them
into the hands
of your
most liberated self.
it will not
put the pieces
back together.
no. no.
it will purify them
in the crucible of surrender
and send them
out into
the world
to love a thousand souls.
p.s. if you ever want to put
the pieces back together again,
don't.
but if you really, *really* want to try,
i may know where one piece is.
go.
take a peek in the mirror
and you will see what i mean.

once a pebble
then you cracked me open
embraced my imperfections
swallowed my fears
and now i am the space
between those broken pieces.

don't be scared
of being broken.
it's one sure
way of opening
yourself up
to the everything.

i fell
within myself
and landed
flat inside
the heart
of the universe.

poof!

and that
wasn't the
end of it.

in no time,
before i
could recover,
the universe
swallowed me up.

and just
like that,
i was gone....

so, now
i cannot
find myself
inside the
vastness
of itself.

only the
universe is there.

to choose love
over everything,
is to
be tempted
by the
darkest of nights.

do not
be tempted.
for within
that choice
lives the eternal.

Ever bright
Ever burning
Ever loving
Ever present.

Why keep looking
For the light you already are?

hurt and fear are twin fires
we pass through to get to liberation.

do not ignore them.

but the more you feed them,
the more you burn.

instead, fill your water buckets with
forgiveness and compassion,
then keep moving forward.

deepening

have you heard?

all of humanity
is enveloped in love.
resistance is futile.
you cannot escape it.
so don't even try.

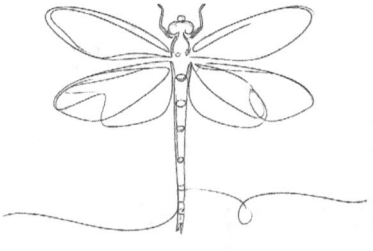

step inside
the world
of your neighbors,
through the
door of tenderness.

be a tree,
a toad.

a mackerel,
a mountain.

a daisy,
a dragonfly.

be a hive.
be humanity,
a portal for love.

in just a moment,
the purest
vision of love
we see
inside ourselves
will take form
through our words
and deeds.
wait …
for …
it …
no.
that is not
how it works.
we must
give love
to make
it real.

standing in
the infinite
ocean of love,
i look around—
and there you are.
coloring your hair
while editing
your video
to post on
your youtube channel.
i walk
towards you
and you
hold out
your hand
and blow
me a kiss.
i catch it
and send you
a giant one
right back.
and it
dawns on me:
i am here
with you,
my son,
standing in
love together.

i am
in love
with my son.
i continue
walking on.
now aware
that i am
completely soaked
from the drop
of ocean
inside your
air kiss.
interesting …
this ocean's water
is not salty,
not at all.
it's marmaladey,
the taste
of love.

listening.
listening.
listening …
listening deeply
to the frequency of life.
listening …
until
the listener,
the frequency,
and life
are one.

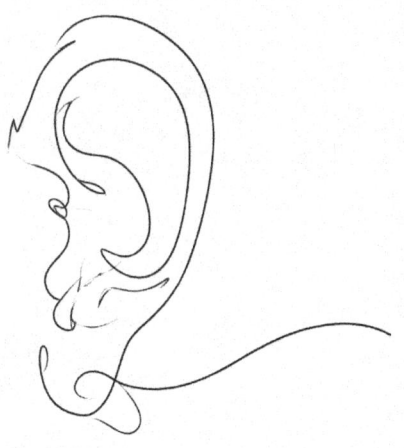

sensing my expansive self,
how can it
fit inside my mind?
my mind tries to control it by
thinking it down into small bits of
identities
that it wishes to bind and devour,
though its efforts are futile
because my identities are safely
held in the bosom of the immortal
expansive self.

be careful of thinking
that your life could
possibly be governed by
the ideas and behaviors of others.

you are not depressed
because your father
abandoned you decades ago.
you are not a terrible person
because your partner said so.
you are not not in the
job you want because
your government has not created it.

life has one cause.
and that cause places no limits on man.

that cause is love.

know of anyone who has
accomplished great things
despite being abandoned,
judged,
or neglected by their government?

you are the effect of love.
period.

be careful of the cause you choose.

you don't need more time with god.
you need more god in the time you already have.

some people confess that
they could spend more time with god.
god is always around.
he is reflected in all:
in the melodic chirping of the birds,
in the never-ending waves of the ocean,
in the disarming smiles of your children.

there is neither space
nor time
where god is not.

begin to recognize
god in all things,
and your time will become infinite.

when you've
been presented
with a
new life,
been remade
anew,
find a
perfectly good
enough mind
and heart
surgeon
to remove
any attachments
to the
mind and
fears from
your heart.
while they're
at it,
have them
brighten the
light inside you.

i know
the best
surgeon, in
case you're
looking for
a referral.
the divine
is the
best i
know. she
has performed
too many
of these
surgeries to
count.

don't ever
think small
of yourself
now, or
later.
for you
are the
heart of
love, the
purest note
in the
divine's sacred
song.

if you're
feeling stuck,
unable to
move,
check if
you have
tied yourself
up,
anchored yourself
with cords
of guilt,
regret and
shame.

if so,
get something
super sharp
and cut
yourself loose.

p.s. if you're wondering what tool would
be sharp enough, try gratitude.
if that's a little dull, although i doubt it,
try acceptance.
if that doesn't do the job, pull self-love
out from its sheath and slice away.

don't go
looking too
far.

no need
to leave
where you
are, physically
at least.

no need
to run away.

stay there.

stand unmoving.

for you
are the
pot of
gold at
the end
of the
rainbow.

you.

when you
get home
and walk
out of your
shoes and
leave them
at the
door, or
anywhere you
feel like …

thank you!

i find
so much
joy inside
the sole
of them.

i guess
this is
how the
divine feels.

me walking
around,
just leaving
her love everywhere.

if you become
quiet enough,
you will feel
the rhythm
of your own thoughts.
move beyond the rhythm
and you will
end up in a
dance with god.

last night
when you
told me
"i. love. You."

my soul
became endlessly calm.
it is
not that
you haven't
said those
words before.
you have.
maybe a hundred times now.
but this time
when you
told me,
it was
as though
you paused time,
quieted my mind,
held the
face of
my soul
in the
palms of
your hands
and kissed it.

and my whole
body became light.
honestly, i don't think
i can handle this again.
once is enough.

we billions must dig
an infinite well
where compassion
and grace flow freely
for that time when
our unfolding love
for each other
opens up old wounds
that may cause
us to leak out
the very essence of
our being.
then one of us
can dip that bucket
of awareness deep inside
that well of grace
and offer that hurting one
a drink....
a holy nectar that replenishes
and patches us up
to be love again.

yes,
pray 5 times a day
hold the 7th day holy,
and the 1st too.
and all the rest.

walk to a sacred site
at least twice.
hug some trees along the way.
fast.
be sober.
be celibate.

and if you can't
keep that thing to yourself,
then marry,
but do not divorce.
obey the golden rule
and the 10 commandments.

know the 4 noble truths
and the 72 names for god
or is that 650?
whatever the number,
remember to use a capital letter.

and then,
when you've done all that,
stop.

celebrate.
if you're not in heaven yet,
then be done with it all.

give it all up.

break all those rules to pieces.

cease your obedience.

and only then,
may you see god's face
shining through your
sinful happy heart.

as the birds
sing and dance
to the rhythm of life,
i accompany them
when i sit still and love publicly.

we all play our part.
i love you.

human love
is hard
to find.

i thought.

so, i
turned to
the divine:

please, you
must now
be my
love,
partner,
and mate.

and then
he directed
me towards
you.

who would
have thought it?
the divine
outsourcing her
love to you.

one question for you:
how much
did she
pay you?

knowing her,
i bet
she gave
you everything.

even when "lost" in a crowd,
feeling hurt by another,
or being grilled
in the boardroom
for a "mistake"
you cannot escape.

you are constantly
in love's crosshair.
you are love's target.

her eye is on you even now.
gotcha!
happens all the time.

now, go out into
the world knowing that
love's got you marked.

what else could you
add to your favorite beach,
the cherry blossom tree,
the rainbow lorikeet,
or the misty mountain
to make them more beautiful and
perfect?

then, what would make
you think that you are
incomplete,
imperfect,
or a work in progress?

you get no credit
for what is already
more perfect
and beautiful
than your strange thoughts
would have you believe.

so, back off.
just a little.
leave the majesty
that you are alone.

we have
turned the
mind into
god. no
longer do
we consult
the oracles,
the dragon
bones, the
voice in
the wind,
or the
photos in
dreams.

the directions
of spirit
have become
foolishness. and
the mind,
most wise
and divine.

we now
turn to
the mind
to make
sense, to see.

what do
you think
i should
do next?
we ask.

can the
mind discern
the future?
through what
eyes does
it see?

we make
a god
of falsity
and ignore the

one who
made us,
gave us mind,
eyes, tongue, heart.

listen,
i cannot
abandon the
infinite one

to follow a
god only
as big
as me.

so, i'll
keep looking
to the
rainbows, talking
to the
trees, offering
flowers to
the waters,
and bending
my knees.

farewell mind
god, may
you rest
in peace.

being with
me will
crack your
heart wide
open.

loving me
will make
you scream
from the
top of
pleasure's mountain.

and what a
lovely climb
it is.

your yes
to loving
me unconditionally
will be
the portal
we walk
through to
inhabit the
kingdom of
the divine.

and as
we live
as divine
beings, playing
a human
game, we
will love
each other
irrationally, make
magic easefully,
and dance
gracefully, like
bodies of
light in
god's hands.

walk gently upon the earth.
i have countless siblings
who live low,
expressing their wisdom
about being grounded.
so, please.

watch your step.

i stepped outside the bubble
of my own creation
and landed in a world
of countless projections.
now, i am wading
through worlds
following the scent of
love's liberation.

read aloud
what's written
on the pages
of every soul
you meet
and one
day soon
you will be
fluent in love.

whether for
one minute,
one hour,
or one day,
sitting on our
meditation cushion
prevents violence,
preserves lives,
and lovifies
our one
human heart.

forgiving yourself
and others
is like unclogging
the vessel that is you,
to allow love to
flow uninhibited.

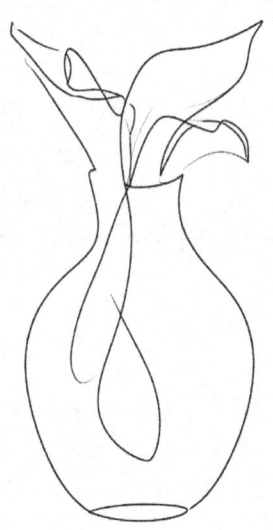

the stream of life
flows,
engulfing the material,
and cuts mercilessly through
the spiritual.
what can stand
in the path of
life's singular
purpose of oneness?

i tried to contain
love's ever-expanding fluidity
with my mind
and i could not hold it in.

so, i apologize in advance
when it spills all over you.

what is the length
of your love?

wrap it twice
around the
one that annoys
you most
and it reaches
to infinity.

do not think on this.
just start wrapping.

if you want to count
the number of years
since our love started,
then you
must break
it down to a
single unit.

then include
all the
times we
traveled with
the stars,
died in
each other's
arms, and
became shards
of thoughts
flying out
from the
divine's mind.

and then
you must
factor in
the distance,

and track the
speed of
the pieces
just before
they re-form again.
yes.

that's the number.

from the spaciousness
of the self,
reach into the
groundedness of life.
then drop all reaching.
be life itself.

there is
a tree
in every religion.
yet, no man
worships the tree.

we praise
the ones
who sat
underneath them,
on them,
and talked
to them.

even baby jesus
was cradled
by one
that someone
chopped up
and then
named it: "manger."

all this
to say:
"it's the tree,
you idiots."

teaching us
to stand
in the now,
while reaching
for god.

no, there
are not
multiple forms
of love.
there is
only one:
unconditional.

the universe is hosting
a "show some love"
party for everyone,
everywhere today.
admission is free.

there will be lots of
dancing and loving.
you do not want to miss it.
judgment and doubt are not allowed.
(they tend to crash these events.)
bring understanding and
trust to have a good time.
see you there!

i walked for a thousand years
to unlock the heart
and let my wisest self in.
now, i sit like a rock
to keep the door wide open
for just one more moment.

i love you
is now
grammatically and
universe-ally
incorrect.

truer to say:
everything loves
everything.

i know.
it's a
mouthful.

i suppose
that's the
intention.
for our
mouths to
be filled
with love.

acknowledgments

it is nice to swim around in the ocean of love. what's even nicer than that is swimming around with others. i am grateful to be a human being and to be in good company as i float through this life. i am grateful for my floating partner, julia, who is way more grounded than i am. love, thanks for reading my poems, improving on them, and inspiring others. being with you "a-mused" me (i hope you can tolerate this one dad joke). thanks for being in this ocean of love with me.

i have chosen this path of love, of obedience to the divine. i'm going everywhere it flows. i suppose this book is a kind of declaration of obedience. and it would still be unborn if not for the consistent prompting of my long-time assistant, samantha francis, who kept nudging (and sometimes poking) me to publish some of my poems. big thanks to you, sam.

sage, you are truly that. it's been a delight swimming in this infinite ocean of love and words with you. thank you for saying yes to helping this accidental poet put this book out into the world. you are a joy to work with.

i must also thank all the mystics, saints, and yogis
who showed up to help me at various points along
this submersion. their lives have been a great source of
guidance. a thousand thank yous to you, who have been
reading and commenting on my poems since 2016. you
helped me feel less alone swimming around in the
cosmic ocean. thank you.

finally, infinite thanks to that "wise old man" who
transcends time, space, and culture, and who is the
best that i am.

about the poet

as far back as he can remember, akasha has been in love with the divine. he sought after god among the trees, the stars, in sacred texts and through plants, in monasteries, in solitude, in community, and in his own heart. everywhere he looked, god was there. his most joyful moments come from spending time with god and experiencing the magic of falling upward and inward into her embrace. you don't want to see the state of his meditation cushion. it is well used and loved.

home for akasha is in the infinite ocean of love. and he
enjoys squatting on various places on the earth. one
of his favorite places is grenada in the caribbean—his
homeland.

akasha thinks of himself as an accidental poet. writing
poetry started out as a part of his spiritual practice.
in 2016, as a way to deepen his listening to the divine,
he would sit in silence, quiet his mind, listen beyond
listening, and then write whatever message would come
from the emptiness. many of them turned out to be
poetic. he now calls this practice "soulalogue." what you
hold in your hands now is a collection of soulalogues
with the divine.
in addition to soulaloguing, or writing poetry, he serves
as a developmental leadership coach and facilitator to
leaders all across the world. he partners with them to
cultivate their capacity for deeper awareness and leading
from wholeness. serving his clients is a sacred practice.

his other passions are many. they include being in
ceremony and dancing wildly, communing with nature,
laughing with life, surrendering his surrender, looking
beyond what the eyes can see, listening to waves crash
against rocks, feeling himself breathing, and simply
being alive.

his greatest hope is that these poems become a hand that gently opens the door of your heart a little wider for you to experience a splash from, or better yet, a complete submersion into, the infinite ocean of love.

https://linktr.ee/drakasha
if you enjoyed this book, please consider leaving a five-star review on amazon, and sharing the book with others who would enjoy a deep dive into love. thank you so much!

love everything!

www.ingramcontent.com/pod-product-compliance
Lightning Source LLC
Chambersburg PA
CBHW060044150626
46556CB00018BA/2689